THE UNIVERSE

Mars

Revised and Updated

Tim Goss

Heinemann Library
Chicago, Illinois

Customer Service 888-454-2279

Visit our website at www.heinemannraintree.com

Photo research by Mica Brancic
Designed by Richard Parker and Tinstar Design www.tinstar.co.uk
Illustrations by Calvin J. Hamilton
Printed in China by Leo Paper Group

12 11 10 09 08
10 9 8 7 6 5 4 3 2 1

New edition ISBNs: 9781432901660 (hardback)

9781432901783 (paperback)

The Library of Congress has cataloged the first edition as follows:

Goss, Tim, 1958-

Mars / by Tim Goss.

        v. cm. -- (The universe)

Includes bibliographical references and index.

ISBN 1-58810-912-7 (HC), 1-4034-0613-8 (Pbk)

1. Mars (Planet)--Juvenile literature. [1. Mars (Planet)] I.Title. II. Series.

QB641 .G68 2002

523.43--dc21

2002000814

Acknowledgments
The author and publisher are grateful to the following for permission to reproduce copyright material: pp. 4, 6, 9B, 16, 19, 24, 28 NASA/JPL/Caltech; p. 5 NASA; p. 7 NASA and the Hubble Heritage Team (STScl/AURA) ; p. 8 PIRL/University of Arizona/NASA; p.9T NASA, James Bell/Cornell University, Michael Wolff/Space Science Institute, and the Hubble Heritage Team (STScl/AURA); p.10 Lowell Georgia/Corbis; p.11 NASA/Space Telescope Institute; p. 12 NASA/U.S. Geological Survey; pp. 13B, 21 NASA/Ames Research Center; pp. 14, 15, 17, 20, 29 NASA/JPL/Malin Space Science Systems; p. 18 Steve Lee/University of Colorado, James Bell/Cornell University, Michael Wolff/Space Science Institute, and NASA; p. 19 Courtesy of Calvin J. Hamilton/www.solarviews.com; P. 21T Bettmann/Corbis; pp. 22, 23 NASA/Kennedy Space Center; pp. 25, 26 Science Photo Library/NASA; p. 27 NASA/JPL-Caltech/Cornell

Cover photograph by Getty Images/Digital Vision

The publishers would like to thank Geza Gyuk of the Adler Planetarium for his assistance in the preparation of this book.

Contents

Any words appearing in the text in bold, **like this**, are explained in the Glossary.

Where in the Sky Is Mars?

If you look up at the night sky, you can sometimes see a brightly glowing red **planet**. This is the planet Mars. Mars is the fourth planet from the Sun. Its neighbors are Earth and Jupiter. Like the other planets, Mars moves through the sky from night to night. The best time of night to see it depends on the time of year.

Mars is one of the eight planets in our **solar system**. It is one of the four planets in our solar system known as the Rocky Planets. The other three are Mercury, Venus, and Earth. Mars is the farthest Rocky Planet from the Sun.

This photo of Mars was taken by the Hubble Space **Telescope** in 1997.

Why is it called Mars?

When people looked at Mars long ago, its red color made them think of blood and wars. They thought that the planet was like a strong soldier who was always ready for battle. For that reason, the ancient Romans named the red planet after Mars, their god of war.

The solar system

The solar system is made of all the planets, **comets**, and **asteroids** that circle the Sun. The Sun's **gravity** pulls on all of the objects in our solar system. If it were not for the pull of the Sun, the planets would travel in straight lines. This would send them out into deep space! The force of gravity keeps the planets in regular paths around the Sun called **orbits**.

Mars comes close to Earth

Mars is the fourth planet from the Sun. It is between Earth and Jupiter.

Sometimes Mars and Earth are close together as they orbit the Sun. This happens about every two years and two months. Mars is opposite the Sun in the sky at this time, so it is said to be in **opposition**. Mars comes particularly close to Earth about every 15 to 17 years.

The time it takes a planet to rotate one time around its **axis** is called a **day**. Like Earth, Mars needs about 24 hours to rotate one time. The time it takes for a planet to orbit the Sun is called a **year**. It takes Mars about 687 Earth days to orbit the Sun. This means that a year on Mars lasts almost two Earth years.

Why Does Mars Look Red?

Mars is often called the Red Planet because it shines with a red-orange light in the sky. Up until a few years ago people used to wonder why Mars was red. In the 1960s and 1970s, the National Aeronautics and Space Administration (NASA) sent **space probes** to Mars. They found out that Mars is red because of rust in the **planet's** soil.

Over millions of years, water and oxygen in the **atmosphere** of Mars soaked into the rocks and started **chemical reactions** with the rocks and dust. This could have happened because Martian rocks and dust have a lot of iron in them. Iron is a metal. When a rock with iron in it mixes with water and oxygen, the chemical reactions make rust. Over time, almost all of the oxygen in Mars's atmosphere was soaked up by the rocks of Mars to make rust. Now there is so much rust staining the rocks and dust of Mars that the entire **planet** looks red.

This was the first color picture taken of the surface of Mars. You can see how red the soil is.

How Is Mars Different from Earth?

Mars is about half the size of Earth and much colder. There is no rain to water plants or air for animals to breathe, so there is no life on Mars. There are no oceans on Mars or dirt that would be the right kind for growing plants. Mars has lots of rocks and no trees. Seasons last twice as long because a **year** on Mars is twice as long as Earth's. There is not enough oxygen in the air on Mars for humans to breathe.

Mars is colder than Earth

Mars and all of the **planets** in our **solar system orbit** around the Sun. The Sun supplies almost all of the heat energy to the planets. The farther a planet gets from the Sun, the colder it gets. Mars is much farther away from the Sun than Earth, so Mars receives less heat.

Mars also loses heat easily because it has a very thin **atmosphere** compared to the Earth. An atmosphere works sort of like a blanket. Earth has a thick atmosphere that keeps it warm, while Mars's thin atmosphere lets the heat out quickly. During the winter months, temperatures on Mars can be as low as −189°F (−123°C). This is 60 degrees colder than the coldest temperature recorded on Earth. During the summer months, temperatures on Mars can climb as high as 63°F (17°C). This would feel like a spring day on Earth.

This picture of Mars shows some of its frosty, white water-ice clouds.

You could not breathe on Mars

Our **atmosphere** on Earth has many gases. It contains a very important gas called oxygen. We need oxygen to breathe. The atmosphere of Mars does not have enough oxygen gas for humans to breathe. Astronauts would need special space suits with oxygen tanks to explore the **planet**.

Clouds on Mars are made of water ice and reddish dust particles. Dust storms on Mars have been known to stretch across the whole planet and last for months.

When Mars first formed, gases were trapped inside the planet's atmosphere. Over millions of years, many of these gases slowly escaped into outer space. Much of the oxygen that was in the atmosphere is now in the form of rust or frozen water. There are no plants or other life forms on Mars to produce more oxygen. The atmosphere of Mars now is mostly made up of carbon dioxide gas. This is the gas that humans breathe out. The air on Mars is so thin, it would be impossible for us to breathe there.

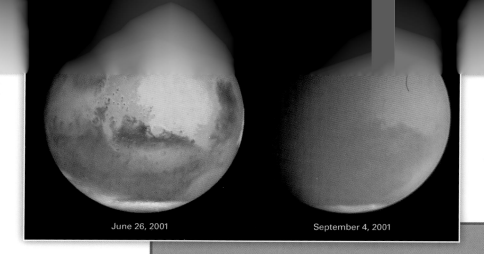

June 26, 2001

September 4, 2001

The image on the right shows how completely a dust storm once covered Mars. The details of the planet that we can see in the image on the left are completely hidden by the storm.

Mars has bad weather

Space probes to Mars have taught us that Mars has thin clouds, high winds, and huge dust storms. These dust storms can be 5 miles (8 kilometers) high. During a **day** on Mars, the temperatures change a lot. The average daytime temperature on Mars during the summer is −10°F (−23°C). The temperature at Vanda Station in Antarctica on Earth gets up to 59°F (15°C). That is much warmer than an average day on Mars. The average nighttime temperature on Mars during the summer is −135°F (−57°C). Temperatures on Mars change more during just one day than temperatures on Earth change during whole seasons!

A photo of the surface of Mars shows that there is a thin coating of ice on the rocks and soil.

What Would I See if I Went to Mars?

If you stood at the north or south pole of Mars, you would see lots and lots of ice. The north half of the **planet** also has flat desert areas. The south part of the planet has deep canyons. Across the planet, there are also tall cliffs, huge **volcanoes**, dried-up riverbeds, and huge holes in the ground called **craters**.

It always looks like winter at the poles

Imagine placing a giant belt around the middle of a planet so that the top and bottom parts are equal sizes. The top half is called the planet's northern **hemisphere** and the bottom half is called the southern hemisphere. The imaginary "belt" on the planet is called the **equator**.

The area at the top of the northern hemisphere is called the north pole. The area at the bottom part of the southern hemisphere is called the south pole. Each of these places on Mars has long seasons of very little sunlight. During those winter seasons, gases in these areas get very cold and freeze into a type of ice. Each hemisphere on Mars, like Earth, has a polar cap.

The *Viking* **lander** and its **rover** collected samples of the soil on Mars for scientists to study.

This is a huge piece of ice that covers part of the planet's surface. Just like on Earth, the ice caps on Mars grow each **day** during the winter as more and more ice forms. However, on Mars, this ice is frozen gas as well as frozen water.

Are Mars's ice caps different than Earth's?

Mars has two ice caps—one at its northern tip and one at the southern tip. Scientists think that the ice caps are mostly made of frozen carbon dioxide gas. This is the gas that humans breathe out. Carbon dioxide ice is much colder than the water ice that makes up Earth's ice caps. Scientists have also found some frozen water ice in Mars's northern ice cap.

Summer on Mars

Suppose you place a tray of ice outside in the sunlight. If the outside temperature is warm enough, the ice will quickly disappear. This is because the heat energy from the Sun's light rays melts the ice. Something like this happens on Mars. As a Martian polar cap gets more light during the summer, the heat energy raises the temperature. The ice caps shrink as their edges boil away in the form of carbon dioxide gas.

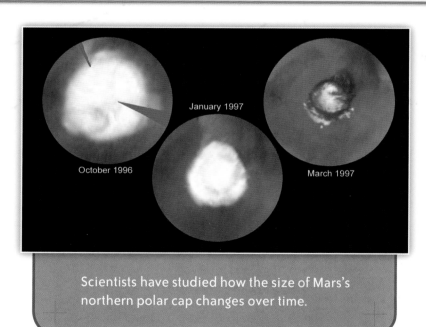

October 1996

January 1997

March 1997

Scientists have studied how the size of Mars's northern polar cap changes over time.

Canyons and craters

The canyons of Mars are long, deep cuts in the surface that stretch for many miles. The largest group of canyons on Mars is called the Valles Marineris, or Mariner Valley. It was named after the spacecraft that first photographed it—*Mariner 9*. The canyons are about 6 miles (9.7 kilometers) deep and 400 miles (644 kilometers) across. It takes more than six hours to travel 400 miles in a car on a highway.

On some parts of Mars you can find groups of large **craters**. Scientists believe that long ago the surface was hit by a series of huge rocks from outer space called **meteors**. Rocks that crash into a **planet's** surface are called **meteorites**. When huge meteorites crashed into Mars, they exploded, making craters in the surface of the planet. These large meteorite impacts, or crashes, can create stronger explosions than any nuclear explosion.

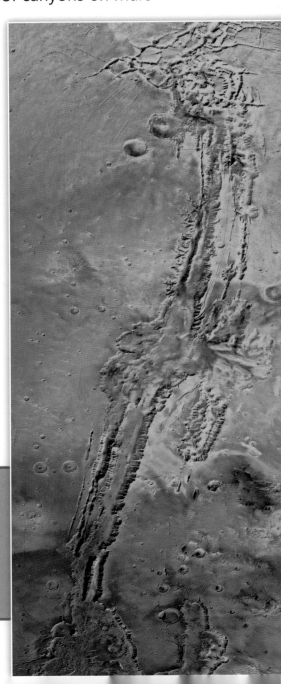

Mariner Valley is the length of the entire United States. If the separate canyons were placed end to end, they would stretch much further.

This Martian meteorite was found on Earth in 1996.

What has come to Earth from Mars?

Scientists who study Mars have been very lucky. Small rocks from Mars have actually fallen from the sky and landed on Earth. These rocks are called Mars meteorites. They were blasted from the surface of Mars by a huge meteorite impact, or crash. These rocks got thrown off the planet and into space at speeds of many miles per second.

Out of the many thousands of meteorites discovered, only a few dozen are from Mars. Meteorites from Mars have been found all over the world. Most of them landed in places like Antarctica, the Sahara or the Arabian deserts, but some have been found in more populated areas like Indiana, Brazil, and France. Scientists hope to learn more about the surface and **atmosphere** of the Red Planet by studying these meteorites.

Mars has volcanoes

When Mars first formed, the inside of the **planet** was very hot. High temperatures inside Mars caused the rocks to melt and form **magma**. Massive streams of magma flowed upward toward the surface. The melted rock exploded onto the surface of Mars.

When magma reaches the surface of a planet, it is called **lava**. Long ago, lava on Mars poured out and spread across the planet's surface. As it slowly cooled, the lava changed back to solid rock. Huge mountains of cooled lava, called **volcanoes**, formed on the surface.

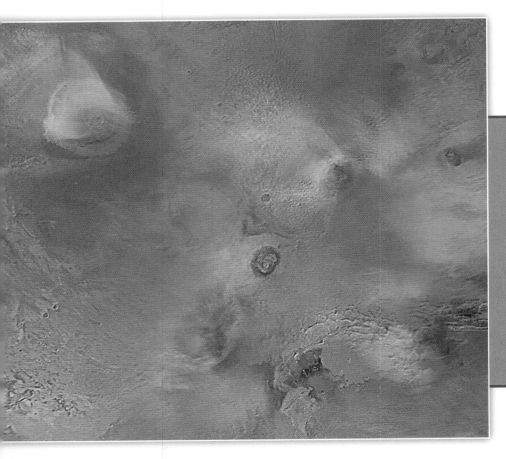

Most of the volcanoes on Mars are found in a part of the northern **hemisphere** called the Tharsis Region. The region stretches about 5,000 miles (8,000 kilometers).

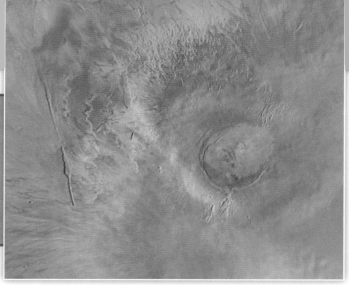

Mount Arsia, shown here, is one of the largest known volcanoes. Only Mount Olympus is larger.

The four largest volcanoes on Mars are named Mount Olympus, Mount Arsia, Mount Pavonis, and Mount Ascraeus. There is no sign that any of the volcanoes will erupt again, but scientists are not certain.

Mount Olympus is the tallest volcano of any planet in our **solar system**. It is more than 15 miles (25 kilometers) high and 435 miles (700 kilometers) wide. It is three times as tall as Mount Everest, the tallest mountain on Earth. It is also wider than the country of England. The last major eruption was about 200 million years ago, but smaller eruptions took place less than 2 million years ago.

This photo shows what Mount Olympus looks like from about 560 miles (900 kilometers) above the surface of Mars.

Looking up at the moons of Mars

If you were on Mars, you would have to be near its **equator** to see its two **moons**. Each Martian moon is a lump of rock only a few miles across. The moons **orbit** Mars much more closely than our Moon orbits Earth. If you went too far toward the north or south pole, though, you would not see the moons. This is because Mars's moons orbit the **planet** near the equator.

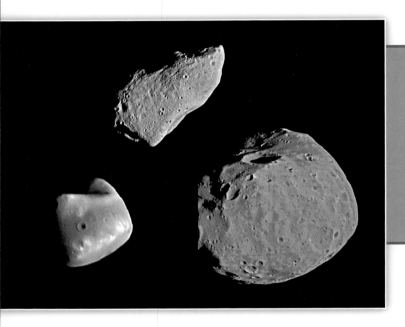

In this collection of images, an asteroid (top) is compared to the moons of Mars. Deimos is at the lower left corner, while Phobos is at the lower right corner.

An **astronomer** named Asaph Hall discovered the moons in August 1877. He was using a **telescope** at the U.S. Naval Observatory in Washington, D.C. The moons looked like tiny specks of light. Hall could tell they were moons because they were slowly orbiting the planet.

The moon closest to Mars is called Phobos. It is also the larger of the two moons. It orbits quickly, circling Mars about every eight hours. Scientists predict that Phobos will crash into Mars in only a few tens of millions of years. That is a short period of time in the history of the universe.

The other moon that orbits Mars is called Deimos. It is more than twice as far away from Mars as Phobos. Deimos completes an orbit of Mars about every 31 hours. A spacecraft orbited Deimos from a short distance to photograph it. The photos of Deimos show that the moon is coated in dust.

This is a photograph of Mars's moon Phobos.

Both moons are potato-shaped rather than round. We know about their shape because of photos taken by spacecraft sent to Mars. Scientists believe that these two moons were once **asteroids**. They were probably pulled into Mars's orbit by the force of the planet's **gravity**. Both moons have many **craters** from being struck by **meteorites**. Scientists believe the moons may be as old as Mars itself.

What Is Inside Mars?

Beneath the surface of each Rocky Planet are layers called the **core**, the **mantle**, and the **crust**. **Space probes** that we have sent to Mars have taught us a lot about what the inside of Mars is made of. But we still need to learn a lot more about our neighbor **planet**. Future space probes will probably help us understand more about the inside of Mars.

The core

The center of a planet is called the core. Although scientists are not completely sure, they think that the core of Mars is like the Earth's core. It is probably made up of mostly iron, with a little bit of sulfur. Scientists have not yet been able to estimate the temperature of the core of Mars. They also cannot be sure of the exact size of the core. They think that Mars's core is very hot and probably solid.

This image of Mars focuses on the Tharsis Region, where the planet's largest **volcanoes** are found.

Imagine you were traveling from the center of Mars to the surface. You would travel about 1,000 miles (1,609 kilometers) through a sea of **magma** before finally leaving the core. One thousand miles is a long way! If you were in a car on a highway, it would take you more than fifteen hours to travel that far.

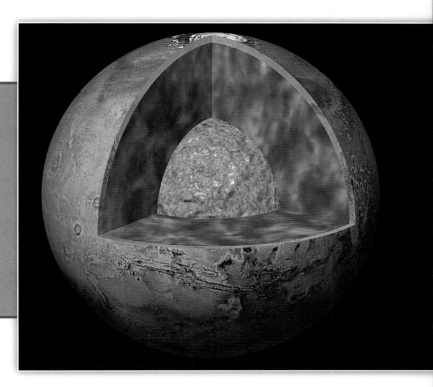

Scientists estimate where each layer of a planet begins and ends. This helps them learn more about the planet. This illustration shows where Mars's layers might begin and end.

The mantle

The next part of the interior of Mars is called the mantle. It is shaped like a thick ball that covers the core. It is made mostly of solid rock, but it can bend like plastic. The rock in the mantle can bend because the temperatures are very high. To pass through the mantle, you would have to travel almost 1,000 miles (1,609 kilometers).

The crust

The last part of your trip would be very short. The outside layer of Mars is called the crust. The crust of a planet acts like an eggshell. It is thin compared to the core and the mantle. It is also hard and it covers everything inside. The crust of Mars sits on top of the mantle and is made of solid rock. The rust-red rocks of Mars make up the outside part of the crust, called the surface.

Is There Life on Mars?

If there is life on Mars it must be very different to life on Earth. The conditions on the surface of Mars are very harsh. There is no oxygen, it is drier than any desert on Earth, and there is radiation from the Sun that would kill most living things. If there is any life on Mars it would have to be very small and live far underground.

People used to think there was life on Mars

More than 100 years ago, an Italian **astronomer** named Giovanni Schiaparelli studied Mars with his new **telescope**. Schiaparelli saw many lines crisscrossing the **planet**. He called these lines *canali*, which is the Italian word for channels. Some people who read reports about the lines on Mars began to think that Mars really had canals. They thought that very smart creatures must have built the canals. Maybe there was alien life on Mars!

For almost 100 years, people still believed there were "canals" on Mars. But starting in the 1960s, scientists from the National Aeronautics and Space Administration (NASA) and other space agencies have sent **space probes** to **orbit** and even land on Mars. Pictures and data from the space probes show that there are no canals and no signs of life on the surface of the planet.

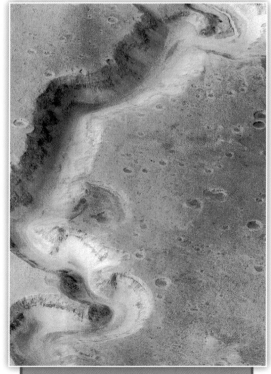

Even the largest canyons on Mars would have been too small for Schiaparelli to see with his telescope.

Were aliens attacking Earth?

In 1938, an actor and writer named Orson Welles scared many Americans. He was the host of a radio show in which actors read plays. On Halloween night, Welles and other actors presented a play based on a novel by H.G. Wells called *War of the Worlds.* The novel was about an attack on Earth by aliens from Mars. The show began with what sounded like a real news flash about an attack on Earth. It sounded so real that many Americans really thought it was happening. They were terrified. They thought Martians were taking over Earth!

There may have been life on Mars in the past

There is not any liquid water on Mars now, but there used to be. Photos of the planet show grooves, or channels, in the surface that must have been made by rivers. Mars must have once had a different type of **atmosphere** and different surface conditions to allow for surface water. After studying Martian **meteorites**, some scientists have suggested that there may have been bacteria on Mars billions of years ago. Many scientists disagree, however. No one knows for certain.

HISTORY OF WATER ON MARS
b.y.a.

4.0   3.8   3.5

2.0   1.0   Now

This is a scientist's idea of the history of water on Mars from 4 billion years ago (b.y.a.) to the present time.

Could I Ever Go to Mars?

Have you ever wondered if you could take a trip to Mars? Maybe someday people will be able to catch rides with missions to outer space. On some missions, spaceships just fly by a **planet**. On other missions, the spaceships land. These spaceships do not always have room for people, though, so you would have to plan your trip carefully.

Packing for your trip

If you did go to Mars, you would need a lot of help for your trip. Remember that the weather on Mars can be very cold. You would need a special space suit and an air tank for breathing. Removing your space suit for even a couple of seconds would be deadly! You would also need a spaceship to get you there. Even in a very fast rocket, it would take at least six months or a year to get there. You might also want to bring a small truck called a land **rover** for traveling across the rocky surface. It would be tough hiking around all those rocks, canyons, and **volcanoes**.

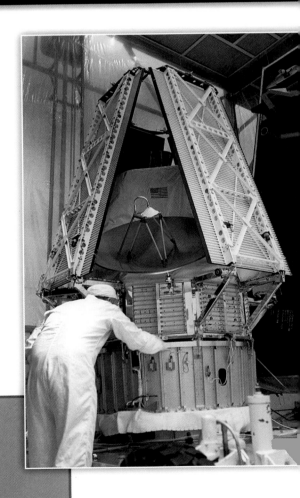

This photo was taken while workers were running final checks on the *Mariner 9* space probe before its launch.

Early exploration

Since the 1960s scientists have been sending **space probes** to study Mars. The first U.S. space probes were the *Mariner* missions. The first three *Mariner* missions were "flybys" which just zipped past Mars without stopping and only photographed a small part of the planet. *Mariner 9* was the fourth and last *Mariner* mission to go to Mars. The probe actually flew in an **orbit** around Mars. From 1971 to 1972 it took more than 7,000 pictures of almost the entire surface.

Mariner 9 is shown here, lifting off and heading for Mars.

Viking Missions

In 1975, NASA sent two space probes, *Viking 1* and *Viking 2*, to Mars. Each *Viking* space probe was made of two important parts. The main ship, called the **orbiter**, circled in an orbit around Mars and took many thousands of pictures of Mars. The second part, called the **lander**, left its orbiter when they were close to the Mars **atmosphere**. The lander went down through the atmosphere of Mars to the surface of the planet.

The *Viking* landers were like small science stations. They had mechanical arms to scoop up rocks and dust from the surface. They also had cameras and small machines to study the surface, soil, and atmosphere. They tested the gases in the atmosphere, the chemicals in the soil, and took many temperature readings. They finished their work in 1982.

The Mars Pathfinder mission

On December 4, 1996, NASA sent a **space probe** called *Pathfinder* to Mars. *Pathfinder's* trip was very different from previous missions to Mars. It was much smaller than earlier missions and flew straight into the **atmosphere** of Mars, using friction with the atmosphere to slow down. When it fell to within five miles (8 kilometers) of the ground, parachutes opened up. Finally, just before it reached the surface, more than twenty airbags inflated. *Pathfinder* landed on the soft cushion of the airbags. It bounced many times before stopping. After it stopped bouncing, the airbags were deflated and a tiny truck called a **rover** rolled out.

The rover was about the size of a microwave oven. Its job was to travel over the surface to places out of the reach of the **lander** and test the rocks of Mars to see what they were made of. During the three months that the *Pathfinder* mission lasted, the main lander and the rover were able to send back hundreds of pictures and test dozens of rocks.

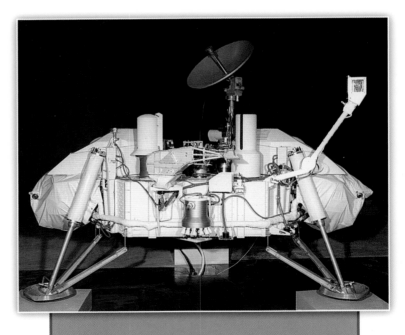

This is a photo of the *Viking* lander that was on the surface of Mars.

There is also a fleet of space probes looking down at Mars from space right now just like the *Viking* **orbiters** did years ago. NASA and the European Space Agency (ESA) have sent four different spacecraft, *Mars Global Surveyor, Mars Reconnaissance Orbiter, Mars Express Orbiter,* and *Mars Odyssey* that are all **orbiting** Mars today. They are studying different things, taking amazing pictures, measuring the chemicals in the rocks and air and even looking for underground ice. The *Mars Reconnaissance Orbiter* has cameras so powerful that they can see things smaller than a person. They've even taken pictures of the landers and rovers on the ground. By the time you read this there will probably be even more spacecraft orbiting Mars!

An artist's conception of the *Mars Reconnaissance Orbiter* (MRO) in orbit around Mars. The MRO will take the most detailed images ever seen of the surface of Mars.

Exploring Mars is hard!

Controlling a complicated space probe from millions of miles away is difficult! Not all the space probes that scientists have sent to Mars have been successful. Some, like the Russian *Mars 96* probe, have blown up during their launch from Earth. A few missed Mars completely and flew off into space. Others have landed on Mars, but only lasted a few seconds. One probe, the *Mars Climate Orbiter*, crashed into Mars because programmers forgot to change units from feet into meters! But even the failures teach scientists something and each probe is better than the ones before. We are learning more and more about Mars!

Mars Exploration Rovers

One of the most amazing missions to Mars are the two Mars Exploration **Rovers**, *Spirit* and *Opportunity*. *Spirit* and *Opportunity* were launched on June 10 and July 7, 2003 and landed on Mars on January 4 and January 25, 2004. After the success of the *Pathfinder* mission, scientists wanted to have a much bigger rover on Mars that could carry out more experiments and travel much further. *Spirit* and *Opportunity* are about the size of a golf cart and carry five different scientific instruments. They were supposed to last for 90 days and travel a few hundred yards, but more than 1,000 days and five miles (8 kilometers) later they are still going strong! No one knows how much longer they will last.

The two rovers have discovered amazing things. They have sent back many thousands of pictures and measured the chemicals in hundreds of rocks. From the pictures and the samples of the rocks, scientists can tell what Mars was like billions of years ago. Scientists think that the area that *Spirit* is driving in was once a lake!

The Mars Exploration Rovers are exploring the surface of Mars. They have already lasted more than 12 times as long as was expected, and have traveled over 5 miles each.

Driving a rover on Mars is a lot harder than controlling a remote-control car. It takes many minutes for a signal to travel from Earth to Mars, so every movement has to be very carefully planned. The MER rovers have special computers on board so that they can do some of the driving themselves, but humans have to decide every step.

This is a picture of Husband Hill on Mars, taken by the Mars Exploration Rover *Spirit*. It was named in honor of the astronaut Rick D. Husband, commander of the Space Shuttle Columbia during its tragic last mission. Husband Hill is about 350 feet (107 meters) tall.

Future missions

Mars is one of the most exciting **planets** for us to explore. So much about Mars is a lot like Earth, but so much is completely different! Plans for future Mars exploration include more **orbiting space probes**, more rovers, and even airplanes and balloons. Sometime soon NASA plans to start designing and building the space craft to send astronauts to Mars. Maybe you'll get to be one of the first explorers to step foot on Mars.

How did the *Pathfinder* rover get its name?

NASA asked American schoolchildren to choose the name for the special Mars rover. They named the rover *Sojourner*, after Sojourner Truth. She was a famous African-American woman who fought for the rights of slaves and women in the United States. The word *sojourner* means "explorer."

Fact File

	MARS	EARTH
Average distance from the Sun	142 million miles (228 million kilometers)	93 million miles (150 million kilometers)
Revolution around the Sun	1.9 Earth years	1 Earth year (365 days)
Average speed of orbit	15 miles/second (24 kilometers/second)	18.6 miles/second (30 kilometers/second)
Diameter at equator	7,521 miles (12,104 kilometers)	7,926 miles (12,756 kilometers)
Time for one rotation	24 hours, 37 minutes	24 hours
Atmosphere	carbon dioxide, nitrogen, oxygen, water vapor	oxygen, nitrogen
Moons	2	1
Temperature range	−189°F (−123°C) to 63°F (17°C)	−92°F (−69°C) to 136°F (58°C)

When images of Earth and Mars are placed next to each other, we can see that Earth is much larger.

A trip to Mars from Earth

- When Mars and Earth come closest to each other in their **orbits**, they are 35 million miles (56 million kilometers) apart.

- Traveling by car at 70 miles (113 kilometers) per hour would take at least 57 years.

- Traveling by rocket at 7 miles (11 kilometers) per second would take at least 58 days.

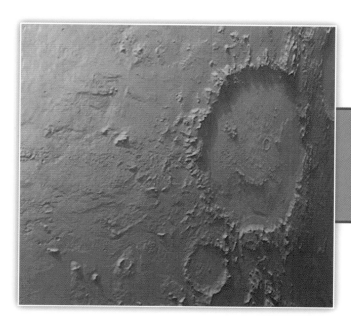

One of the **craters** on Mars looks like a happy face!

More interesting facts:

- A person who weighs 75 pounds (34 kilograms) on Earth would weigh about 29 pounds (13 kilograms) on Mars because of the difference in **gravity**.

- There are inactive **volcanoes** on Mars that are larger than the state of Arizona.

- NASA plans to send humans to explore Mars.

Glossary

asteroid large piece of floating rock that formed at the same time as the planets and orbits the Sun

astronomer person who studies objects in outer space

atmosphere all of the gases that surround an object in outer space

axis imaginary line through the middle of an object in space, around which it spins as it rotates

chemical reaction when two or more different chemicals mix and cause a physical change

comet ball of ice and rock that orbits around the Sun

core material at the center of a planet

crater bowl-shaped hole in the ground that is made by a meteorite or a burst of lava

crust top layer of a planet that includes the surface

day time it takes for a planet to spin around its axis one time

equator imaginary line around the middle of a planet

gravity invisible force that pulls an object toward the center of another object in outer space

hemisphere one half of a round object in space

lander small spaceship that lands on the surface of a planet or a moon

lava melted rock from inside a planet or moon that pours out onto the surface

magma melted rock inside of a planet or moon

mantle middle layer of a planet or moon. It lies between the core and the crust.

meteor piece of rock or dust that travels in outer space

meteorite piece of rock or dust that lands on the surface of a planet or a moon from space

moon object that floats in an orbit around a planet

opposition opposite position in the sky than the Sun when viewed from Earth

orbit curved path of one object in space moving around another object; or, to take such a path under the influence of gravity

orbiter spaceship that flies in orbit around a planet

planet large object in space that orbits a central star, has an atmosphere, and does not produce its own light

rover small truck that is used to study the surface of a planet

solar system group of objects in space that all float in orbits around a central star

space probe ship that carries computers and other instruments to study objects in outer space

telescope instrument used by astronomers to study objects in outer space

volcano mountain built up from layers of hardened lava

year time it takes for a planet to orbit the Sun one time

More Books to Read

Eckold, David. *The Ultimate Mars Rover*. New York: Dorling Kindersley, 2004.

Feinstein, Stephen. *Mars*. New Jersey: Enslow, 2005.

Ward, David. J. *Exploring Mars*. Minneapolis: Lerner, 2006.

Index